Acknowledgments

I want to thank my incredible Creator and Redeemer for making this amazing world and allowing me to share it with others. I am very thankful for my wonderful and loving family for always being there for me and helping me every step of the way. I want to extend appreciation to Dr. Mark Whalon and Dr. Jonathon Schramm for their feedback and advice. I want to thank John Dykstra, who took many of the beautiful photographs in this book and who glorifies God with his art. A huge thank-you of deep appreciation goes to my editor and collaborator, Mary Hassinger, who has also become my friend.

ZONDERKIDZ

Wilderness Discoveries
Copyright © 2011 by Peter Schriemer
Photos © 2011 John Dykstra, gettyimages, istockphoto, almay photos

Requests for information should be addressed to:
Zonderkidz, *Grand Rapids, Michigan 49530*

ISBN 978-0-310-72142-0

All Scripture quotations, unless otherwise indicated, are taken from the Holy Bible, *New International Version*®, *NIV*®. Copyright © 1973, 1978, 1984, 2011 by Biblica, Inc.™ Used by permission. All rights reserved worldwide.

Any Internet addresses (websites, blogs, etc.) and telephone numbers printed in this book are offered as a resource. They are not intended in any way to be or imply an endorsement by Zondervan, nor does Zondervan vouch for the content of these sites and numbers for the life of this book.

Editor: *Mary Hassinger*
Art direction: *Cindy Davis*
Interior design: *Brand Navigation*

Printed in China

11 12 13 14 15 16 /GPC/ 10 9 8 7 6 5 4 3 2 1

the nature of GOD

Wilderness Discoveries

To the Creator, who sends the snow in winter,
the summer warmth to grow the grain, the breezes,
the sunshine, and the soft refreshing rain.
—P. S.

"The power of God is present at all
places, even in the tiniest leaf ... God is
currently and personally present in the
wilderness, in the garden, and in the field."
—Martin Luther

Introduction

I was excited. In just a moment the bald eagle would take flight and soar along the coast of Lake Michigan. Months ago, someone had found it sick and weak. Some kind people, who were trained to help birds of prey, rescued the bald eagle and nursed it back to health. When the eagle was strong enough, it practiced flying in a large flight cage. Now the eagle was ready!

People were gathered around, watching and waiting. Cameras were ready and so was I! Then it happened. The woman holding the eagle gently threw it into the air. The eagle opened its huge wings and flew across the water. My eyes never left it as it gracefully headed down the coast of Lake Michigan. God must have enjoyed creating such a beautiful and awe-inspiring creature.

God has blessed me with many amazing wildlife experiences, but they didn't happen by sitting at home—I had to get outside so God could show me his incredible natural world. My goal is not only to help you understand the majesty and creativity of our great Creator, but also inspire you to explore and experience the nature of God for yourself.

—Peter Schriemer

What Is an Ecosystem?

Have you ever wanted to see where a river goes or find out what's on the other side of that next hill? One of the reasons God made this earth was for us to have fun exploring and discovering it! God has filled the natural world with amazing animals and plants that make our adventures exciting and interesting.

When you walk out your front door, you are entering an ecosystem! The word "ecosystem" is used to describe areas of the natural world. Sunlight, air, water, plants, and animals are parts of an ecosystem. Within every ecosystem, each plant and animal is designed to serve a specific purpose in God's creation. In an ecosystem, animals and plants live in ways that keep things in a certain balance that make it possible for life to flourish.

Ecosystems can be large areas. Lake Michigan, northern wetlands, and forests are all examples of ecosystems. Within these big areas, creatures make their homes in smaller spaces called habitats.

Habitats Provide Creatures with:

- Oxygen (in the right amounts)
- Suitable Temperatures
- Food
- Water
- Shelter
- Area to Raise Young

As an adventurer, you'll explore ecosystems, discover habitats, and encounter the amazing creatures living there.

Lake Michigan Dune Ecosystem

"How **precious** to me are your thoughts, God! How vast is the sum of them! Were I to count them, they would **outnumber** the grains of sand..."

PSALM 139:17-18

The Great Lakes

There are five Great Lakes. You can remember their names if you think of "HOMES": Lake Huron, Lake Ontario, Lake Michigan, Lake Erie, and Lake Superior. The Great Lakes have more fresh water than any other place in North America!

The Great Lakes are shared by Canada and the United States. Michigan is surrounded by the Great Lakes and has more freshwater coastline than any other state. If you lined up Michigan's coastline, it would stretch from the tip of Florida all the way to the state of Washington!

With so much freshwater, the Great Lakes region has many ecosystems with lots of creatures. Let's take a look at the beautiful sand-dune shoreline of Lake Michigan.

HURON

ONTARIO

MICHIGAN

ERIE

SUPERIOR

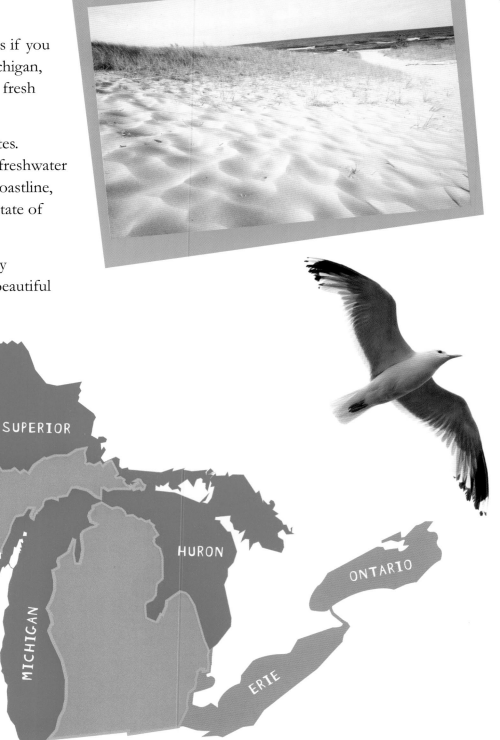

The Dune Ecosystem

The smooth sand along the beaches of Lake Michigan is made of finely ground-up minerals—mostly quartz. Wind off the lake blows the sand around, making drifts and mounds called dunes. The sand will keep blowing around unless there's something to keep it in place.

When a plant called marram grass begins to grow in the sand, the dunes grow bigger and can stay in place for a very long time. When this happens, other plants can grow on the dunes too. Older dunes may even have huge forests growing on them! This creates habitats like the sandy beach, the grassy foredune, and the forested backdune.

Wildlife living on the beach looks for food in the morning and finds shade during the hottest part of the day. Creatures in the foredune get some shade under the marram grass, and animals in the forest have shade all day long.

Each species deals with the unique conditions on the dunes, thanks to God's great plan.

Are you ready to go on a treasure hunt along the beach in search of God's amazing creatures? It's time for some wild discoveries!

Marram grass

 **HELLO, MY NAME IS:** This is called the "ant lion" because when it is young, it's a ferocious predator ... of ants!

Ant Lion

Most ant lions are diggers. They make cone-shaped pits in the sand to catch their food. The ant lion buries itself at the center of the pit and waits to surprise insects that walk by. If an ant or other small insect doesn't fall in, the ant lion throws sand to knock it down into the pit. The shape and design of the pit keeps the insect from crawling back out as the ant lion throws sand to create landslides.

Once the insect is at the bottom of the pit, the ant lion uses large jaws and poison to keep the prey from escaping. After an ant lion has captured its food, it doesn't actually eat it! It sucks out all the juices! Yuck! When it's done drinking, it throws the body out of the pit.

Ant Lion Hole

The scientific name for tiger beetle is "cicindela" (sis-in-dela), which means "glow worm" (even though it doesn't glow and it's not a worm)! It is called a "tiger" beetle because it is a predator and has tiger-like stripes.

Tiger Beetle

With big eyes and jaws, fast running legs, and speedy wings, tiger beetles are excellent hunters. When a tiger beetle catches an insect, it doesn't really eat it. Similar to the ant lion, it chews the insect and sucks out the juices. It's like putting all your food in a blender and drinking it. Sound tasty? Tiger beetles don't even drink water. They chew wet sand or soil to get a drink.

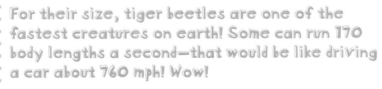
For their size, tiger beetles are one of the fastest creatures on earth! Some can run 170 body lengths a second—that would be like driving a car about 760 mph! Wow!

Crazy Cool FACT!

The Fowler's toad was named in honor of American wildlife naturalist S.P. Fowler. He was the first to see that this toad was a different species from the American toad.

Fowler's Toad

Fowler's toads have several ways to take care of themselves. God gave them the ability to blend in with their surroundings. We call that **camouflage**. They can bury themselves in the sand or soil to hide, or they can play dead. If all that doesn't work, they've got one more trick up their toad-sleeves …

The Fowler's toad has two glands behind its eyes that have poison in them. Don't worry, if you handle one gently you have nothing to worry about, but predators that bite them have to watch out! The milky white poison tastes awful and may make the predator sick.

It's NOT true that you can get warts from a toad. Warts are really a virus—ewww! The bumps on a toad's body help it blend in with its natural surroundings.

Crazy Cool **FACT!**

 Poison gland

[HELLO, MY NAME IS:] The hognose snake gets its name from its pig-like upturned nose. That nose helps the hognose snake burrow into the soil.

Eastern Hognose Snake

The eastern hognose snake prefers habitats with lots of toads. Hognose snakes will eat small mammals, birds, and some insects, but their favorite meal is toads! Even though toads have those poison glands behind their eyes, hognose snakes produce a special substance in their bodies that allows them to eat as many toads as they want!

When the hognose snake is threatened by a predator, it can pretend to be a venomous snake—like a cobra! It may coil up, inflate its head and neck, and strike! It may also flip upside down with its mouth open—pretending to be dead.

 Crazy Cool **FACT!**

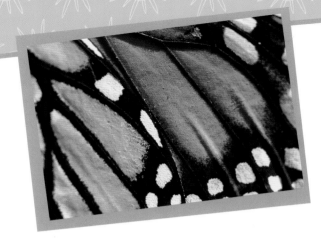

Early European settlers were impressed by the beauty of the monarch butterfly and named it "monarch" (which means king) after King William, Prince of Orange.

Monarch Butterfly

Monarch butterfly moms lay small eggs on milkweed plants found in the marram grass on the foredune. The milkweed stems and leaves are food for the young caterpillars. Milkweed plants are poisonous to many creatures, but God designed monarch caterpillars so that the poison doesn't hurt them. Instead, it makes the monarch poisonous to other creatures. Pretty neat!

In the animal world, bright colors often say: "I'm poisonous—don't eat me!" Monarchs can be easy prey. That's why God designed them with bright colors to tell predators they would NOT be a good meal.

Caterpillars go through one of the biggest changes of all— metamorphosis. The caterpillar hangs upside down, sheds its skin, and reveals a chrysalis! Inside the chrysalis, God not only gives it a new wardrobe, but a new body as well! After a couple weeks inside the chrysalis, out pops a new creation—a beautiful butterfly!

Another amazing thing about the monarch is what it does as an adult. Monarchs that were born late in the summer begin to gather together in August. These butterflies fly more than a thousand miles south, to Mexico! Here they stop in the exact same area every year and rest until spring, when they fly north again.

It's a mystery how every year monarchs find the same place to hibernate in Mexico! Why do they go to that spot? How do they find their way back? God designed them to do all these things. Scientists are still trying to figure it out!

Crazy Cool FACT!

[HELLO, MY NAME IS:]

When threatened by a predator, a box turtle pulls its head, tail, and legs inside its shell. A hinge on the bottom of its shell allows it to close up after it pulls inside. The predator is left with nothing but a hard shell that looks like a box!

Eastern Box Turtle

Can a turtle leave its shell behind, like cartoon turtles sometimes do? Reach behind yourself and feel your backbone. Can you leave your backbone behind? No, and neither can a turtle. A turtle's backbone is actually part of its shell.

Box turtles love sandy forest areas like the backdune, where they can find and eat plants, earthworms, slugs, and insects. When creatures eat both plants and animals like this, they're called omnivores.

When winter comes, the box turtle digs down into the sand and dirt to stay until spring. It is like a long deep sleep. God designed the box turtle so it can freeze solid in the winter and be just fine when it thaws out in the spring!

Box turtles can live a long time. Many reach 40 or 50 years old. One box turtle that was kept in captivity lived to be more than 130 years!

Crazy Cool FACT!

The great horned owl gets the name "great" from being one of the largest owls in North America and "horned" from its tall ear tufts that kind of look like horns.

Great Horned Owl

God designed most owls to be nighttime hunters! Owls have specialized ears that hear the smallest noises. Their ears also help them locate exactly where their prey is moving. Once they have heard a noise, owls have amazing eyes that can see long distances and in very low light.

When flying through the air, owls hardly make a sound. Why? Specially designed feathers, of course! The front of their wing feathers are serrated like a comb, while the back of their wing feathers are frayed like the fringe on a scarf. This cuts down on wind resistance and the noise the wings make. God designed owls just right for silent flight in the stillness of the night.

Great horned owls are one of the few creatures that will eat a skunk. Having no sense of smell, they don't mind dining on stinky skunk once in a while!

Crazy Cool FACT!

Transition Forest Ecosystem

" . . . For every animal of the forest is mine, and the cattle on a thousand hills. "

PSALM 50:10

Transition Forest Ecosystem

There are many forests across America. Each one has a distinct set of trees, plants, and creatures living in them. **Broad-leafed trees**, like maple trees, are common across the east and the south, while forests in the north are mostly made up of needle-leafed trees.

Many broad-leafed trees can't survive north of the Great Lakes. At the same time, many needle-leafed trees need colder temperatures and usually don't do as well south of the Appalachian Mountains. So in the **Great Lakes region**, you have **transition forests**. Here, broad-leafed and needle-leafed trees live in the same ecosystem, as do creatures and plants from the south and the north.

Within a forest ecosystem, there are many habitats where creatures can live. There are places under logs, in wetlands, and up in many different kinds of trees.

Click beetles get their name from the clicking sound they make when they launch themselves into the air.

Click Beetle

This little beetle may not look like much, but never underestimate God's creatures! The click beetle has a very flexible area near the middle of its body with a spine and a pit. The beetle also has very strong muscles that allow it to do something spectacular.

If the beetle is stuck upside down or caught in a bird's mouth, it arches its back and snaps the spine into the pit! The powerful muscles pop the beetle into the air, away from danger. Some click beetles can launch themselves up to five inches off the ground. That's like you jumping 30 feet into the air from lying on your back!

Though click beetles live in the forest, the easiest way to find them is around outside lights at night.

Click beetles are the natural world's fastest accelerators. This means they can go from standing still to moving at high speeds quicker than any other animal!

Crazy Cool FACT!

Red-backed salamanders have a rust-red stripe down the middle of their backs, which is where they get their name. Some are gray colored and are called lead-backed salamanders.

Red-Backed Salamander

During the day, they hide from predators under logs or dead leaves. After it rains, everything is nice and wet, which is the perfect time for salamanders to go out and hunt. Red-backed salamanders eat mites, millipedes, beetles, spiders, and ants … just to name few.

God gave red-backed salamanders an **amazing way of communicating.** They leave **scent marks** that other salamanders smell. These scent marks tell other salamanders the boundaries of a salamander's territory, the size of the salamander that left the scent mark, and the identity of the salamander! That's amazing!

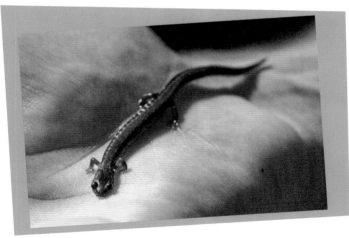

Crazy Cool FACT!
Did you know that red-backed salamanders don't have lungs? How do they breathe, you ask? Through their skin!

Dinner, anyone?

Garters are elastic straps that some men used to hold up their socks. They were often brightly colored, just like the bright stripes on the garter snake.

Garter Snake

Garter snakes have **great camouflage**! When a snake has patterns on its body, like the stripes of the garter snake, it makes the snake harder to see. This helps it hide from predators—like hawks, herons, and foxes. It also helps them hide from small animals that they hunt—like earthworms, salamanders, and insects.

God also designed the garter snake's camouflage to **help it escape**. It can be difficult to catch them! The stripes make it harder to see where they're moving as they quickly slither through grass and leaves.

Great camouflage

Did you know that snakes smell with their tongues? A snake's tongue can actually sense what's in the air. It's kind of like tasting what everything smells like.

Crazy Cool FACT!

The Latin name of the gray tree frog is "Hyla versicolor." "Hyla" means "belonging to the woods." "Versicolor" comes from words "versi," which means "various," and "color," which means ... "color." This tells us they can change color and that they live in the woods.

Gray Tree Frog

When it comes to hiding, gray tree frogs are experts! They have excellent camouflage. God gave these tree frogs special skin that allows them to actually change color! They can be shades of green, gray, and brown.

A forest is great for gray tree frogs. There are many places to hide during the day, lots of insects to eat at night, and wetland areas for laying eggs. On summer nights, you can hear them in the trees above your head.

Similar to the box turtle, gray tree frogs can freeze solid in the winter. Their bodies make a substance that keeps them alive, even when their brain and heart stop for short periods. In the spring, the tree frog thaws out and is ready to go again.

Crazy Cool **FACT!**

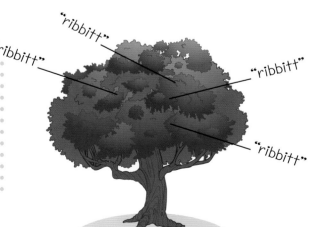

"ribbitt"

"ribbitt"

"ribbitt"

"ribbitt"

[HELLO, MY NAME IS:]

Red squirrels get their name from their reddish-brown fur. They are sometimes called pine squirrels, because they eat seeds from pinecones. Their Latin name means "the steward who sits in the shadow of his tail"!

North American Red Squirrel

God created red squirrels for life in the trees. Their hind feet rotate backward for climbing down tree trunks. They have special whiskers that help them maneuver as they jump and run among the branches.

That's not all! They also have big eyes to watch out for predators and help them see as they scamper through the trees. These squirrels also have a great sense of smell for finding food, even after they've buried it underground or in a tree!

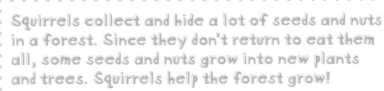
Squirrels collect and hide a lot of seeds and nuts in a forest. Since they don't return to eat them all, some seeds and nuts grow into new plants and trees. Squirrels help the forest grow!

Crazy Cool FACT!

Walking sticks are part of the order Phasmida, which in Greek describes something that seems to appear out of nothing.

Walking Stick

Walking sticks have great camouflage. They sometimes seem to appear out of nowhere when they begin to move! They are created to look exactly like part of a tree. The shape and colors of their bodies make them look like stems and their legs like twigs. When walking, they move slowly and pretend to be a stick blowing in the wind.

Without this protection, they would be much easier for birds and other predators to find for lunch. They blend in so well, it's almost impossible to find them in a tree—but you might spot one on the side of a building.

Found it!

If a walking stick loses a leg in a struggle, it is OK! Young walking sticks can re-grow legs as they get bigger.

Crazy Cool FACT!

HELLO, MY NAME IS:

The eastern hemlock is found in eastern North America. Some people thought it smelled similar to a completely different European plant—the poison hemlock—so it was named eastern hemlock.

Eastern Hemlock

Hemlocks are slow-growing and long-living trees. It may take 300 years for one to reach full size, and it can live for more than **800 years!** Forests that have large hemlocks have been around a long time.

Eastern hemlocks are good for animals. They provide shelter and bedding for white-tailed deer in the winter. Their dense branches provide important shelter for squirrels, ruffed grouse, turkeys, and other animals. Their seeds also provide food for wildlife.

Crazy Cool FACT!

Unlike the poison hemlock of Europe, the eastern hemlock can be used to help people. The twigs and leaves have been used for making a tea and medicine for people who are sick or hurt.

The red-shouldered hawk's name comes from the rust-red feathers in its upper wings that make it look like it has reddish shoulders.

Red-Shouldered Hawk

Red-shouldered hawks are designed for life in the forest. First, they have short, wide wings. Why is that helpful? Shorter and wider wings make it easier to fly in between trees. If they had a long wingspan like a bald eagle, they could not do that.

Red-shouldered hawks have eyes that can see very far and very well. As they fly through the forest, they look for small animals to catch for food. When they spot a small creature, they use their big talons, or claws, to grab dinner.

Red-shouldered hawks share the same ecosystems with barred owls. They prefer the same habitats and eat similar animals. The hawk hunts for food during the day, while the owl hunts at night.

Crazy Cool FACT!

Northwoods and Wetlands

"Let the trees of the forest sing, let them sing for joy before the LORD...."

1 Chronicles 16:33

North Woods and Wetland Ecosystems

The northern part of the **Great Lakes region** is part of the **huge boreal forest** of Canada. Boreal forests are made of mostly needle-leafed trees, like pine, fir, and spruce. These trees do well in cooler climates with cold snowy winters. There are more boreal forests in the world than any other land ecosystem.

In this area of the north woods, freshwater is plentiful with rivers, wetlands, and the Great Lakes. Creatures living here need to be able to survive harsh winters and short summers. Some stay warm with fur or feathers, some go into a deep sleep, while others migrate south.

Are you ready to explore the north woods and wetlands? It's time for another adventure!

Beavers are rodents like mice and chipmunks. The word rodent comes from the Latin "rodere," which means "to gnaw." All rodents have big front teeth for gnawing on things.

Beaver

Beavers are the **biggest rodents** in North America. Some can get to be three feet long and weigh 60 pounds! They have really thick fur that keeps their bodies dry—even underwater! Beavers have special valves that close to keep water out of their ears and nose when swimming underwater. They also have clear membranes over their eyes that act likes protective swim goggles.

Beavers love ponds, lakes, and streams where they build their lodge homes from trees they cut down with their teeth. Beavers also build dams that can flood part of a forest to make big ponds around their lodge homes. This keeps them protected from predators, like a moat around a castle!

The biggest dam built by a beaver colony is in northern Alberta, Canada. It's been worked on for generations of beavers since the 1970s. It now stretches 2,800 feet and can be seen from space! That's amazing!

Crazy Cool FACT!

This frog is called Rana clamitans, which is Latin for "loud calling." The common name of this frog is the green frog. Why? Because they're green of course!

Green Frog

The body of the green frog is designed for life in the water. Long legs for kicking and **webbed hind feet** make the green frog a great swimmer. In the summer, male frogs establish territories in the pond. When frogs make loud calls, it tells other male frogs to stay away and it lets female frogs know where they are.

God has given this frog **great camouflage**. It blends in perfectly with the colors of the pond. When it's in the water with only its eyes and face showing, the green frog seems to disappear.

Frogs close their eyes when they swallow. Why? Their very large eyes push down inside their mouth, which helps to push food down their throat when they swallow. Crazy!

Crazy Cool FACT!

Water striders are part of the True Bug Family: Hemiptera. All true bugs have a pointed beak-like mouthpart that they use to pierce their food.

Water Strider

Water striders are **specially designed** to move around on top of the water. They stay on the water's surface by properly distributing their weight evenly to their legs. To easily move around, God gave them tiny **water-repellent hairs** on their feet. Using their long legs like tiny oars, they seem to skate across the water.

Water striders are predators that hunt for insects on the water's surface. If an insect falls in, it makes tiny ripples in the water. The water strider feels those vibrations through its feet and will skate over to catch dinner.

Water striders communicate by sending little ripples to each other across the water!

Crazy Cool FACT!

The pitcher plant gets its name from the fact it looks like a pitcher and has water inside!

Pitcher Plant

The pitcher plant is carnivorous, which means meat-eating—but don't worry, it only eats little insects! Pitcher plants have big leaves that form a pitcher-like tube that partially fills with rainwater. The colorful leaves and the water attract thirsty insects to the plant.

Once an insect climbs inside, it's in trouble. The slippery sides and the downward-pointing hairs keep the insect from escaping. Once an insect is trapped inside the water-filled tube, the pitcher plant absorbs the insect through its leaves.

Pitcher plants grow in a special kind of wetland called a bog. Bogs are areas of wet spongy ground with water underneath. If someone carefully walks across a bog, the ground bounces!

Crazy Cool FACT!

Yikes!

The name porcupine comes from the Latin words porcus, meaning "pig," and spina, meaning "thorns."

Porcupine

Porcupines will eat just about any part of a tree, including buds, twigs, inner bark, acorns, and leaves. Since their food doesn't run away, porcupines don't have to move very quickly.

Porcupines may be a bit slow, but God has given them an *amazing defense* against predators. If they can't get to a tree in time to escape, the whole backside of the porcupine is covered in **30,000 quills**! It is not true that they shoot their quills. Instead, if the predator gets too close the porcupine swats it with its tail—Ouch!

OUCH!

Most of the time porcupines are up in trees, sometimes as high as 65 feet. Eating different parts of a tree, they can stay up there for days!

Crazy Cool FACT!

[HELLO, MY NAME IS:]

The symbol of the United States got its name from the old English word balde, which meant white! The bald eagle's head isn't featherless—it's covered in white feathers.

Bald Eagle

Bald eagles have **incredible eyesight**. If they could read, they would be able to read a newspaper from across a football field! Using their long six-foot wingspan for soaring effortlessly on wind currents, they can see their prey far below them.

Bald eagles are designed to be **great at fishing**. They fly high above the water looking for fish. When they spot dinner they swoop in and grab the fish using their large, **sharp talons** to hold tightly as they fly to a treetop to enjoy their meal.

Bald eagles build their nest in the same tree every year, making it bigger each time. The biggest eagle's nest on record was 20 feet deep, 10 feet wide, and weighed 4,000 pounds! Wow!

Crazy Cool FACT!

Final Thoughts

I hope you have enjoyed learning about the Great Lakes region and God's creatures as much as I have. Understanding what ecosystems are and how creatures live in them is very important to understanding how God's natural world works. God has called us to be stewards of his creation, which means he has put us in charge of taking care of his natural world. Knowing how to make the right decisions when it comes to caring for creation means knowing the Creator himself and understanding the needs of plants, animals, and ecosystems.

Several of the creatures in this book have been or are currently endangered because people have not been good stewards. Bald eagles, beavers, and pitcher plants are examples of God's creation that have had hard times or are still facing challenges today. As God's children, we need to make sure we make the right decisions about how we live so God can see we are doing our part to care for what he has made.

No matter where you live, I hope you get outside and enjoy the ecosystems and wildlife that God has designed in your area. Join me, and head outside to experience the nature of God!

ENDANGERED
eagles
beavers
pitcher plants